LEARN TO DRAW

DISNEY · PIXAR
FINDING DORY

Illustrated by John Loter and The Disney Storybook Artists

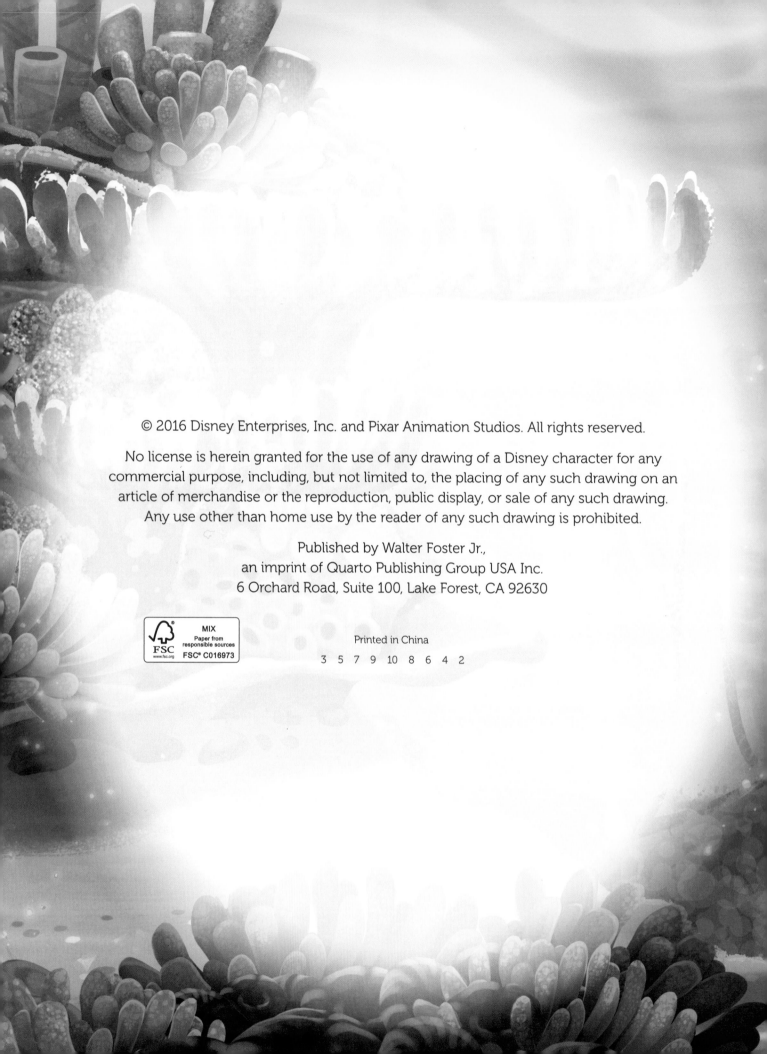

Published by Walter Foster Jr.,
an imprint of Quarto Publishing Group USA Inc.
6 Orchard Road, Suite 100, Lake Forest, CA 92630

FSC
www.fsc.org
MIX
Paper from responsible sources
FSC® C016973

Printed in China

3 5 7 9 10 8 6 4 2

Table of Contents

The Story of Finding Dory

One year after Marlin and Dory's journey across the ocean to find Nemo, the three fish are living happily together as neighbors on the coral reef. As Mr. Ray's new teaching assistant, Dory accompanies Nemo's class on a field trip to watch a stingray migration, where they learn how some animals have a natural instinct to return home. Distracted by long-lost childhood memories, Dory is swept into the undertow. Nemo finds her, disoriented and lying in the sand, mumbling "Jewel of Morro Bay, California." On the way back home, Dory insists she's remembered something important. Nemo mentions the phrase "Jewel of Morro Bay, California," and suddenly Dory has a flood of memories. Dory has a family! She even remembers her parents' names: Charlie and Jenny. After much convincing—Marlin isn't too happy about leaving the reef so soon after their last adventure—Nemo persuades his dad to help Dory find her family, and the three leave the reef together, heading toward the Pacific Coast.

Dory, Marlin, and Nemo meet both old and new friends along their journey, including two righteous sea turtles, Crush and Squirt, who help them surf the currents all the way to California! Dory's not sure where she'll go once she gets there, but she's not too worried—after all, her motto is "just keep swimming!" But after a run-in with a group of local hermit crabs and a giant squid, Dory is scooped up by staffers at the Marine Life Institute, an aquarium in Morro Bay, California, whose mission is to rescue, rehabilitate, and release the coast's sickest fish and sea mammals. Separated from Marlin and Nemo, who've been left outside the Institute, Dory finds herself trapped inside a quarantine tank with a tag clipped to her fin.

Inside, Dory meets Hank, a seven-legged octopus. He reluctantly offers to help her find her parents in exchange for her tag. You see, Hank has one mission: He wants to be transferred to the Institute's much quieter sister facility in Cleveland. Dory's tag is his ticket out.

With the use of his camouflage abilities, Hank sneaks Dory across the aquarium. Finding her parents proves much harder than Dory originally thought, but the closer she gets, the more pieces of her past she uncovers. Along the way, they encounter plenty of distractions—cuddly sea otters and crowded "touch" pools— and an assortment of new friends, including a near-sighted whale shark named Destiny and a self-conscious beluga whale named Bailey.

When Hank and Dory finally reach the Open Ocean exhibit, Hank drops her off and takes her tag with him. Excited, Dory rushes to her childhood home, only to find it empty. A neighboring crab tells Dory that the blue tangs have been taken to Quarantine. The only way to get there without Hank is through the Institute's pipes—a place that frightens Dory. In the pipes, she runs into Marlin and Nemo, who snuck into the Institute with help from a trio of sea lions named Fluke, Rudder, and Gerald and a quirky loon named Becky. They find Dory simply by asking themselves, "What would Dory do?"

Back in Quarantine, Dory, Marlin, and Nemo seek
out Hank, who's about to get on the truck to Cleveland.
He helps Dory find the blue tangs, but they have bad news—
her parents aren't there. Hank scoops up Dory but drops her
when a staffer unexpectedly grabs him. He watches in horror
as she slips through a drain that leads to the ocean.

Dory suddenly finds herself alone and lost outside the Institute.
Just as she's starting to feel overwhelmed, she asks herself, "What would Dory
do? What would I do?" She looks around and spots a trail of shells that lead to her
parents' new home. They've been right outside the Institute all this time, waiting
for Dory! Yet Dory's journey isn't over—Marlin and Nemo are still stuck inside the
truck, on their way to Cleveland with Hank. She has to get them back! With the
help of her new friends and parents, Dory discovers the true meaning of family
and sets off to find Hank and the two clownfish.

Tools & Materials

You need to gather only a few simple art supplies before you begin. Start with a drawing pencil and an eraser. Make sure you also have a pencil sharpener and a ruler. To add color to your drawings, use markers, colored pencils, crayons, watercolors, or acrylic paint. The choice is yours!

drawing pencil & paper

eraser

sharpener

colored pencils

felt-tip markers

paintbrushes & paints

How to Use This Book

You can draw any of the characters in this book by following these simple steps.

Step 1

First draw the basic shapes, using light lines that will be easy to erase.

Step 2

Each new step is shown in blue, so you'll always know what to draw next.

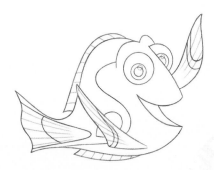

Step 3

Take your time and copy the blue lines, adding detail.

Step 4

Darken the lines you want to keep, and erase the rest.

Step 5

Add color to your drawing with colored pencils, markers, paints, or crayons!

Size Chart

From clownfish to whale sharks,
the ocean is filled with creatures of all shapes and sizes.

Bailey

Rudder   Fluke   Gerald   Otter

Destiny

Becky

Hank

Nemo   Marlin   Jenny   Dory   Charlie

Baby Dory

Baby Dory is wide-eyed, sweet, and a bit forgetful. She suffers from short-term memory loss, which she'll tell you right away—and then promptly forget and tell you again. Years ago, Baby Dory embarked on an adventure that led her far away from her parents and the only home she's ever known.

3

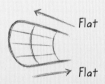

Flat

Flat

Keep the edges of
her fins rather flat,
don't make them
too round

4

She has a round
little nose that
curves inward

7

Dory

Dory has a sunny personality and tries not to let her forgetful nature bring her down. There's only one problem—Dory doesn't remember her family. Of course, she has a new family in her clownfish neighbors, Marlin and Nemo, but something is still missing. Although Dory doesn't quite know what she's searching for or where to find it, she lets her instincts lead the way.

3

From the side, Dory's body is shaped like a football

Dory is just over 4 times the size of Nemo

4

5

Side fins are
straight on top

3 rays

and curved
on bottom

6

From the front, Dory's stripe defines where her "eyebrows" end

Freckles follow the curved bridge of her "nose"

YES! curved freckle pattern

NO! too straight

Charlie & Jenny

Always ready with a joke, Dory's father, Charlie, takes nothing more seriously than protecting his memory-challenged daughter. He teaches Dory how to make the most of life with her short-term memory and how to have a little fun along the way. Jenny, Dory's mother, is a cheerful and caring blue tang. But make no mistake—she is one fierce fish. Her maternal love and wisdom are steadfast, whether she's by Dory's side or an ocean away.

1

Unlike Charlie, Jenny is flat on the bottom and very curvy on top (like a roller coaster)

2

3

Large eyebrows and forehead lines that double as a "comb-over"

Charlie is slightly cross-eyed

4

The nose and mouth shapes for Dory and her family differ:

Jenny   Dory   Charlie

Marlin

Marlin is a not-so-funny clownfish who's been known to go a little overboard on his mission to protect his son, Nemo. But can you blame him? The last time he let Nemo out of his sight, Nemo was fishnapped by a scuba-diving dentist and taken all the way to Sydney, Australia! With Dory's help, Marlin found Nemo and brought him home. Now he's joining Dory on an adventure to find her own family, but first he'll have to get over letting the forgetful blue tang lead the way.

From the side, Marlin is shaped like a turkey drumstick

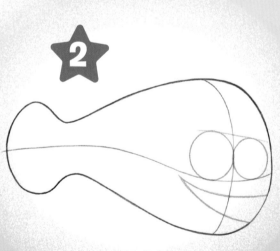

3

Marlin is about 2 times
the size of Nemo

4

Marlin's face is kind of flat

5 rays on side (pectoral) fins and tail

5

6

YES!
eyes close
together

NO! eyes
too far apart

Bags under
his eyes make
him look tired

27

Nemo

After his last adventure, Nemo is back to being a normal clownfish, attending school and living on the reef with his dad and Dory. But after Dory starts remembering pieces of her past and the family she's lost, Nemo wants nothing more than to help reunite them, even if it means crossing the ocean again. He believes in his blue tang friend—he knows what it's like to be different.

From the side, Nemo is shaped like a Goldfish® cracker

From the front, his body looks like a gumdrop

3

YES! top (dorsal) fin is 2 different shapes pointing at different angles

NO! too even; too upright

4

YES! rays follow curve of fin

NO! too straight and even

Top fin is same height as 1 eye

Nemo is about 4 "eyes" tall, including top fin

4
3
2
1
0

YES! bottom fins are set apart from each other

NO! fins look like bow tie

7

Hank

Hank is an octopus living in the Marine Life Institute. OK, technically he is a *septopus*—he lost a tentacle somewhere along the way. But Hank's missing limb has made him no less competent than his eight-legged peers. He has one mission: to be transferred to the Institute's much quieter facility in Cleveland. Despite all three of his hearts, Hank can be a bit of a grump, but even he's no match for one little blue tang's enduring positivity.

3

Keep his eyes on top of
his head, and give him
expressive eyebrows

4

7

Give him a definite
cranium; his mantle
hangs down his back

No need to show all 7
legs in a single drawing
—usually 5 is enough

Destiny

Destiny is the Marine Life Institute's rescued whale shark. She's not too confident in her swimming skills, as her bad eyes make navigating the big blue a challenge. When she was little, Destiny communicated (in whale, of course) with a young blue tang through the Institute's pipes, but when their conversations suddenly stopped, Destiny worried she'd never hear from her friend again.

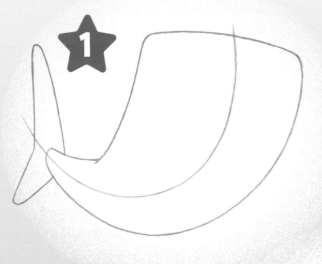

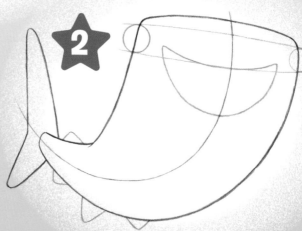

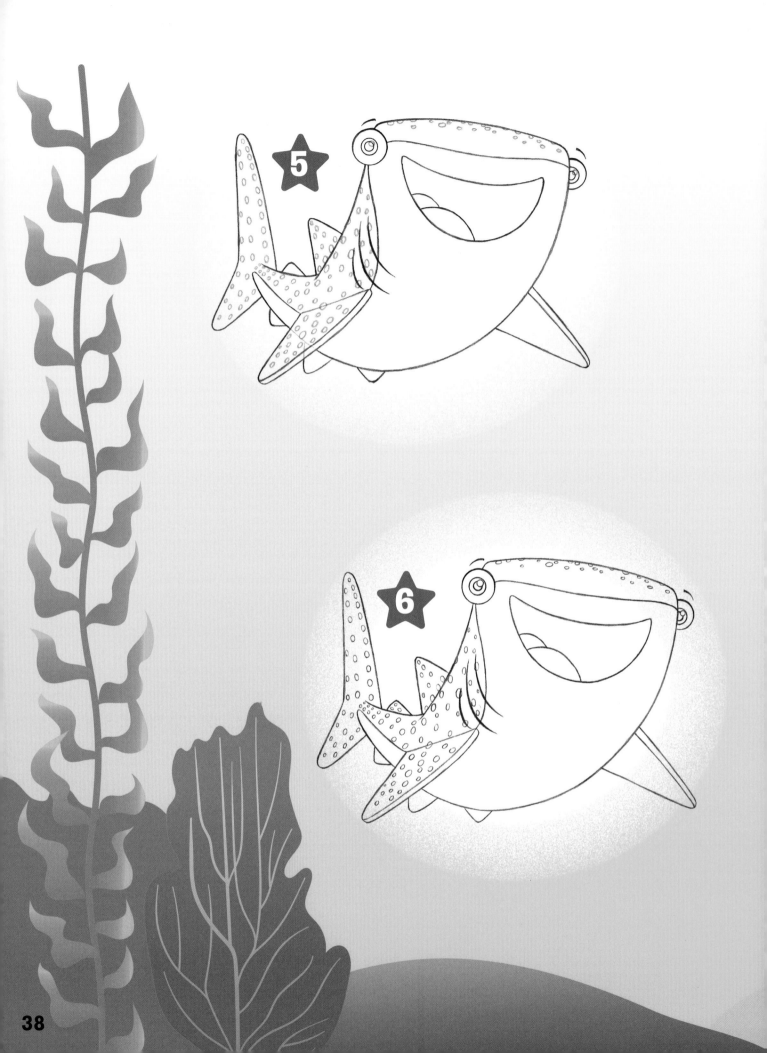

Even though she's as big as a whale,
Destiny's profile is distinctly shark

Bailey

Bailey is a beluga whale living at the Marine Life Institute. He was brought to the facility for a head injury. Though the doctors agree that there is nothing wrong with Bailey, he doesn't believe them for a second. He's convinced the injury damaged his echolocation abilities. Why, just look how swollen his massive cranium is! Of course, the size of his head is perfectly normal for a beluga, but Bailey doesn't know that.

Bailey's head is large, but don't make it...

...too large

...or too small

Aaah, just right!

Fluke

Fluke is a lazy sea lion who spends his days sleeping on a warm rock outside the Marine Life Institute. Fluke shares his rock with Rudder, his pal—but that other irritating sea lion, Gerald, can shove off and find his own!

3

Keep Fluke's shoulders very broad

YES! NO!

4

Rudder

Rudder, another sea lion, is Fluke's best friend. The pair were rehabilitated and released from the Marine Life Institute. Though Rudder isn't interested in leaving his comfortable rock, he and Fluke help Marlin and Nemo get into the MLI by introducing the clownfish to a quirky loon named Becky.

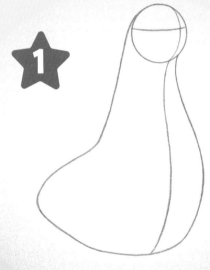

1

2

Rudder's rear fins are rubbery and have 5 individual toes

Draw eyelids that overlap the eye to give it some thickness

Gerald

Gerald is an offbeat sea lion who carries a green pail. All he wants is a seat on Fluke and Rudder's rock, but they're constantly telling him to shove off!

Becky

Becky is a quirky loon who imprints on Marlin. While Becky is a reliable friend, she's also easily distracted—a trait Marlin isn't too pleased about! Carrying Marlin and Nemo in Gerald's pail, she flies the two clownfish into the Marine Life Institute to find Dory.

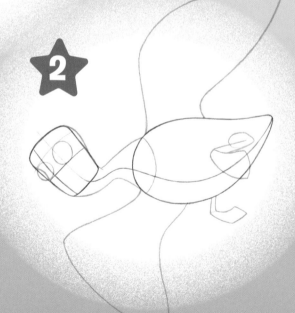

Otters

Adorable and furry, the otters live both inside and outside the Marine Life Institute. They love to hug and frequently have "cuddle parties" that make spectators *oooooh* and *awwwww*. They're so adorable—they literally stop traffic!

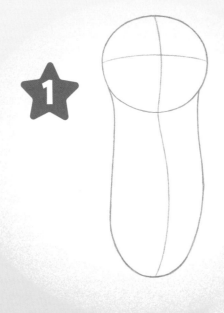

The End